EARTH AGAIN

## MADE IN MICHIGAN WRITERS SERIES

**GENERAL EDITORS**
MICHAEL DELP, INTERLOCHEN CENTER FOR THE ARTS
M. L. LIEBLER, WAYNE STATE UNIVERSITY

**ADVISORY EDITORS**
MELBA JOYCE BOYD
WAYNE STATE UNIVERSITY

STUART DYBEK
WESTERN MICHIGAN UNIVERSITY

KATHLEEN GLYNN

JERRY HERRON
WAYNE STATE UNIVERSITY

LAURA KASISCHKE
UNIVERSITY OF MICHIGAN

THOMAS LYNCH

FRANK RASHID
MARYGROVE COLLEGE

DOUG STANTON

KEITH TAYLOR
UNIVERSITY OF MICHIGAN

A COMPLETE LISTING OF THE BOOKS IN THIS SERIES
CAN BE FOUND ONLINE AT WSUPRESS.WAYNE.EDU

POEMS BY *Chris Dombrowski*

# EARTH AGAIN

WAYNE STATE UNIVERSITY PRESS
DETROIT

21 20 19 18 17                    6 5 4 3 2

Library of Congress Cataloging-in-Publication Data
Dombrowski, Chris, 1976–
Earth again : poems / by Chris Dombrowski.
p. cm. — (Made in Michigan writers series)
Includes bibliographical references.
ISBN 978-0-8143-3729-5 (pbk. : alk. paper) —
ISBN 978-0-8143-3730-1 (ebook)
I. Title.
PS3604.O453E27 2013
811'.6—dc23
2012027176

Publication of this book was made possible by a
generous gift from The Meijer Foundation.

*Typeset by Maya Rhodes*
*Composed in Minion*

*For Dianne Dombrowski and Shirley Burns,*
*and in memory of Dorothy Dombrowski—*
*Mothers*

*And for Luca, Molls, and Fair-Haired Lils*

They are incomprehensible, the things of this earth.
The lure of waters. The lure of fruits.
Lure of the two breasts and long hair of the maiden.

CZESLAW MILOSZ, "The Garden of Earthly Delights"

# CONTENTS

EARTH AGAIN

TABLET

Up the cutbank of a creek named after stone,
striking stone, I came walking, my fingers
stained with the pulp of raspberries picked
from branches arched over descending snowmelt
beneath two clouds and blue sky no one
built. Napped between that extravagant
quilt and sunwarmed sand until the taut line
woke me, tugging in my palm. The trout's
eye was a polished nickel poleaxed
by a drop of ink, though I am writing this
in the brown juice spit from a grasshopper's lips,
instinct having made for many a miracle
such as this emergent mayfly shaking its wings
dry, to whom I whisper—Go light and soft
with this pittance, straight to the lord
whose commandments are writ in water.

## POSSIBLE PSALM

When I saw light the sculptor chiseling sheer bluff
from slope—the cleaved wood landing as shadow
in down-mountain saddles, a coarse grit teasing out
the basalt's facelike features, then finer grains
crazing the air with duff—

I said aloud *good light:* as if it were dog or obedient
child, as if there were some other kind. As if it had not by then
vanished into that antipodal room, the work shrouded in dark sheet.

## SEROTONIN

Afterward he would ask her
what color she saw, what hue

✄

of red if she'd come violently
or green if she'd eased herself down

✄

into that limitless trove
of ecstasies. She'd climb off,

✄

his spent member sliding out
(needle from vein?) and sprawl back

✄

with her hands over her eyes:
I saw white, just white, apples

✄

sliced open, white of moths around
a lamp, my mother's bath towels

✄

folded on a bed. *And you?*

✄

Trout-stirred silt in the clear spring's cress,
the wide meadowstream canopied

✄

by May cottonwoods' full bloom—
not color so much, then, but

≈

a place of vacancy color
might inhabit: what the eyes looked like

≈

before the irises formed,
the river held in cupped hands—

≈

he might have been sleeping by now,
she might have wondered if this time

≈

she would conceive. They would fall
further apart (privacy

≈

of dreams deeper than privacy
of reveries) before dawn's wash

≈

turned indigo the sky above
the cobalt mountains, and she

≈

would draw her hand along the line
day had drawn: the same motion

≈

the womb-child would months later
make against her inner-skin,

little ingot, squinting at
a pale glow just beyond its reach.

Sliding jeans from her hips,
glimpse of an ornate hip-bone
tattoo obscured earlier
by resinous blouse now risen

                           (the moon
a pupil searching out its iris—
which makes the backlit cumulus
a what?)

          The parataxis of her ass,
slight swale of nothing between two hills
before which the nihilist, jubilant, takes vows
interloping between mouth, numen
of stretched neck—

                 no sophistry
her hand driving your head down,
turning you vertiginous:

                  the cloud,
of course, of which the moon
made witness, guest—

## BRIEF DREAM OF BRONWYN RAE

Not that you knew her. Not that what she whispered to me
isn't going to apply: *This might mean more to me
than it does to you.* But what meant anything back then,
at fifteen, when the feared world seemed made of a water

I knew better than to touch, the result of reaching
a damp hand responsible for ruin. And so when
Bronwyn Rae (see, there is absolutely no way you
felt that swift stomach-thump of nerves at the mere mention

of her name as I did) said *touch,* I touched, said *go down,*
I went. Mind you the world was still wet but it fairly
clung to me, my fingers, *lacrimae rarem* to my
tongue. December mendicant, I would have knelt until

my knees bruised but she hoisted me by my drenched armpits,
held me briskly to her then said her mom was coming
soon. Outside, early dark, emberings in the west like
small fires in snow: By which the now-man warms his eyes

(note how quickly if not cumbersomely I've slip-flopped
into third-person-present hoping to hold your ear),
walking home to his own modest house where he would have,
had Bronwyn Rae not found him filching her homework, seen

potential in his otherwise obedient eyes,
likely masturbated and napped before basketball
practice, returned home with testosterone imbued blood
to casually belittle the woman who carried

and pressed him into the world he was now—what? *intrigued*
by, *bestirred?* (And mind you in the poem's present he's still
walking.) Day-thawed, the snow on black branches seizes up,
ensheathing the bare trees turned grand chandeliers dimmed low:

too elegant, sure, but they serve as such a wonderful
fulcrum into the true present: this wintery day
into which I've slept late with your mother, one hand
cupping the smooth globe of her belly and, vaguely, you:

Like me back then (and now if I'm still here) you might have
wondered who you were, assumed you were some general you
to whom the poem had been addressed as I imagined
savoring the dream that transpired in the time I'll

take to punctuate this sentence: Your elbow, perhaps,
or knee nudges briefly the roof of its world and my
stomach does what it did when I didn't so much as
see Bronwyn Rae as sense her palpably in the room.

## POEM WRITTEN IN THE HELIOPAUSE

Now you know completely
all that I've completely forgotten,
foot-drummer, womb-child, high-beam
tracing the curve of the predawn
canyon, cedars and ghost-firs,
the bedrock briefly lit, the seen
seen as through a portal, as when one
shaves layers of frozen lake away
to view the bilious liquid world
below—there are fish and fish
up here called humans though deliriously
we breathe air. Your lungs a month ago
were maple seed pods pinwheeling
toward an asphalt soil: the worried nurses
gestured at a glowing screen. If you'd
been born then, and you weren't,
this might have been your elegy,
maculate, but a sin to speak of now
as your sure pulse caroms against
the faintly lit walls, striations fanning
from the motel door's noon peephole
that is the curtained room's sole comfort.
Or is our planet photographed from
so deep within the cosmos that I fear
both the distance and the dot, though it begs
dimly: *Come nearer, nearer still—*

## EAVESDRIPPING HOUR, SUNDAY AFTERNOON

I'm writing this as if it were happening
right now and it is though there's no way
of accounting on even the most newly fangled
computer program for the legal pad & scrawl
inherited from beloveds—drip, drip, drip-drip
go the holes in the gutter though the squall's
coming sidelong through the sunlight
that shellacs the green plastic turtle sandbox
recently unearthed/unsnowed by a balmy
week along with the toy wreckage of my son
who's napping in his ship-cabin of a room,
dark blue curtains closed, a portal of cyan light
leaking through (cyan his word learned
from a washable Crayola marker) while his
sister nurses, nodding at their mother's breast
on the beige stain-guarded couch near the iPod
playing Evans' Sunday Live at the Vanguard—
Wouldn't it be fabulous to hear some jazz,
I say, on a Sunday afternoon and not Sunday
night so that you wouldn't have to go to sleep
but got to walk around all evening with the music—
but talking to Mary while watching these odd
figures spill out across the yellow paper I've
woken her, though she musters a smile as she
hands me our daughter here three weeks now

and as my narration slips further behind real-time
slaps a slice of bread into the KitchenAid
toaster oven and begins talking into her cell phone
to someone she must know well because I hear
postpartum and not exactly but she wasn't doing well
as I adjust the sidelong cradled girl, her feet
straddling my elbow, warm head in my palm like
a perfect clay cup of tea, her skull's pulsing soft spot
so thin I can see, in the right light, into the sinless
machinery of an infant's brain and immerse myself
in the bath of self-pity I've been drawing
my entire life, but before I can lie down in it
here comes the clap of the boy's bare feet against
hardwood, not the sound of horsemen's stallions'
hooves striking the hardening ground but small
five-toed feet and he's in my lap, latent dreams swirling
behind his eyes asking what are you doing and can you
draw a monster van inside your poem, a monster van
with all four of us inside! And so I do, I draw it but
instead of sketching our faces in the window write
"w/all four of us," ashamed as I am of how much fuel
it would take to get us anywhere in that American
nuclear family carrier and picture the almost-president's
face leering beside video of deteriorating icecaps and know
it's not right to feel this warm on a winter day but I do.

## MY RECENTLY IMPLANTED GOV'T
## ECO GUILT CHIP

is zapping me from a millimeter beneath
the skin at the top of my spine to inform
me that my morning dump, the paper w/ which I
wiped and the flush that sent it all sewerward
has cost the planet six gallons of fresh
aquifer water and two sturdy limbs from a VA
oak forest where formerly ruffed grouse
thrived when acorns abounded. This information
was relayed to me via text message along with
a prescription for a single pill of unknown
pharmaceutical composition which I must
by law ingest before lunch to ensure my brain
chemistry is properly altered and sufficient
feelings of remorse ensue. Since I work at noon
I will have to drive not bike to the pharmacy
thus activating the chip again and triggering
a more potent prescription. It is all enough
to make one cry and being one I do, shedding
ample tears—and reaching momentarily for
a Kleenex before drying my eyes on my sleeve.

IN THE WEEKS BEFORE YOU WERE BORN,
DRIVING THROUGH THE MISSION VALLEY,
HE WATCHES HER BEGIN A LIST FOR LABOR

The way she sips tea: steam, like something conjured,
fascinated by her face. The way the mountains—driving,

watching the sawtooth peaks, he's become distracted by
something, a starling following a small herd of paints
not for the seed unearthed but because tails
festooning in fall light mesmerize—he looks up
and the range has changed shape entirely, a child
growing between blinks. The way a storm-charged creek
doubles sharply back on itself as if to take
a better look at its own swollen figure. The way
will be dark, buoyless and cold, and she will need
gills, sharp constellations, will need a name to call.

The way she licks the pencil's lead, lists *mirror* first:
to see her fingers touch your head, before the final push.

Sudden December cloudlight
pleats the lows where the draw wells shade:
a finger, hawthorn-pricked.
                              The land as handmaid
postulant to herself.
                        Falling to the lichen floor, needles
of larch like so many rings dropped into a prioress's open hand—
*Don't worry, child, no need for those here.*
                                          Not wind
but motherhush stills the renouncing
branches. Not buck but gangly fawn
presses hoofprints into the virgin and virgining snow.

To witness the ten thousand worlds, witness
snow galloping headlong in grains across
drifts of former parasol flakes packed tight
by oak-cracking cold; or the stalled-in-air
leper-skin harried on by gust-flung curds:
each of the countless forms asserting
wordlessly its own distinct name.

                                Such are
the myriad cries of a newborn, waking
(in the hour of vanishing-as-it-lands skift)
to be nursed, or (in the sleet-colored moment
when wind severs cloud and what's fallen
bristles with light) to wonder not where she is
but if.

         Watch her small temples throb, the way
one wail does not reap tears while another,
beginning in her fisted toes, turns skin folds
around her neck into rivers of salt. You
in whose shape she was shaped, whisper
into her ears, once more, that name, single
warm consolation to the cold.

## STRANGE LULLABY

Fire's bride, snow is cold
until it's hot, the drifts

bluish beneath pines that sleep
only on windy nights like this one

with its hailstones galloping
across the hard earth whose depth

Dead Ben measured momentarily
before reporting permanently

to the worms that the flicker craves
all winter—not worms, though,

but jiggers full of sleep that tune
its void-piercing call, its sudden

insistence that it'd been missing,
invisible as a noon constellation

or a woman unstitching, seam
by seam her wedding dress, or god

who never shaves, who has forever
been trying to grow a beard

long enough his mistress the earth
might climb it, hand over hand,

back up to him—its shadow
shrouding her as she trims it

with each new moon.

## NOT KNOWLEDGE

> Memory should not be called knowledge.
>
> *Keats*

### I

My mother's brother's friend: so tall in her memory
he seems as she talks of him like memory itself.
He walked her home a time or two, his brown corduroys
coming together at his knees, the wales scratching out
a sturdy rhythm near her ears (*my ears! He was that*
*tall, I was seven, must have been 'cause I can see*
*Evelyn Street, the sycamore my dad painted white*
*to ward off some bark beetle, the hairy fruits we kicked*
*along the sidewalk. There was never any science*
*behind it, whitewashing the tree, and the beetles came*
*or they didn't . . . God, this must have coincided with*
*the British Invasion!*)—intensely private laughter—
(*Where was I. Oh, the tree. He hacked off a limb or two*
*each year till it was nothing but trunk. Wait, why am I*
*telling you all this?*) Dense pause until we realize,
setting our forks, cups, next to the scramble she has made,
the question isn't rhetorical. But no one says, your
brother's tall friend, your grandson coming down the hallway
wearing new corduroys, their odd knee-made music: we
just sit there watching a willing red rise to her cheeks
like someone summoned to a busy room, then ignored.

## II

Dawn moon staring into and out of the slough, dimming.

First poppy like an offered pill in the backyard's palm.

Quarter falling unnoticed to the bar's boot-scarred floor.

Dipped net pulled up shimmering, apathetic to its catch.

I was telling the bartender about the time I
sawed open a golf ball and nearly lost my eye
to some high-tech liquid gel that shot out from white
dimpled shavings and severed rubber bands with the force
of a thumb-capped faucet, knocking me off the cement
steps—dramatic helpless pose on barstool—my mother
finding me in the geraniums, offending hand
foreshadowing the gauze patch I'd have to wear three weeks,
dreams of starling sorties (my father'd always begged don't
bother the nests, don't bother a mother guarding eggs).

She said: What you needed was an Ativan. Said: Here,
passed a stack of quarters across the liquor-slick bar
and nodded toward the dormant jukebox. I played
B-side Raitt and Dylan—"What's a sweetheart like you
doin' in a dump like this"—and thought maybe she would
tend to me in the hour of my need: her tricep,
halter-top tightening as she poured, maybe she would

proffer some tale of her own, promising orange pill washed
down with something complimentary meant to lure
me a little further toward my ruin. *Hey. Can I—*

You know the line, as hackneyed as the dream when someone
suddenly becomes someone else: cute barmaid now bar-
manager placing his would-be fists on your shoulders,
squeezing gently as the houselights go not down but up.

⤳

You could just start walking, you could walk until dawn,
geese peeling off the sewage treatment settling pond
like a strewn clutch of change, you could picture her by now
at home having showered intricate layers
of smoke from her skin and blonde boy-cropped hair that drips
into the crisp pages of a novel she has pulled
randomly from the bookshelf; you can envision her
staring plaintively at her cell phone and the wrinkled
napkin. . . . But she sleeps with a fastness you can't fathom
or vacuums another powdered line up through her nose
or reads a story to her sleeping son's bedroom door
or goes down once again on her goonish manager for
your tip money, fives and tens. . . . You can cry Call me,
to the high cold stone redux in ditch water, call
me. Will you. Place the washcloth on my clammy forehead.
Mother me. Beg: Little moon, St. Memory, look me
in the eye. As day slips again through night's indifferent
net, comes on without reproach, white and desolating.

## III

Illucid, opaque: the steamy Mason jar dermised
with frog breath and frog piss and sometimes frog turds, the remnants
of crickets and grasshoppers I'd gathered, sacrificed
to my sparsely warted porch-god whose Latin name
*Ascaphus truei* means lacking a body part and
true eye. Sometimes I saw the flexed legs, bow & fiddle,
protruding from the excrement and sometimes heard the
final glass-muted songs (without irony, of course)
but never saw the pink flash of tongue, though once, moment
too late, caught its throat bulging with a still-kicking foot,
true-eyes held wide, deeply sated amidst the sparsest
furnishings: a handful of well-fertilized grass, twig,
parking-lot pebble or two, a sky of cellophane,
two scissor slits for ventilation, perspiring
like a shower curtain.—There. It took some time getting

here: I'm at the top of the shag-carpeted stairwell
about to send some toy-man rocketing down the railing
when my mother steps out of the bathroom and adjusts
her towel—full shot: hair and all. Do our eyes meet? Does
my look of recognition belie my innocence,
reveal I've seen similar in the porn-mag Von keeps
under stacked cinder blocks? No. Not that I remember.

What nourishment, though. What indelible residue.

Up before us always before dawn before a hunt
even winter-wracked as she would get: *Here, my Sonshine,*
*eat this*—heaping bowl of oats—*it will stick to your bones.*

## IV

If not trapped tree frog: Then pelican free-diving
into bluefin harried bait ball, surfacing to gulp,
shiver-down a mullet. And if not pelican then
heron stalking pineshadows for gecko, stilling-up
before the lunge, half-accurate stab: body severed
from still-squirming tail, wriggling consolation the bird
tips down its flute-thin throat. How long does it last, then, this

quivering otherness inside? How long until the tail
tightens, the cricket's instrument's crushed, the minnow
goes stiff inside the womb-dark gullet? Is born again,
say, in white plop beside a tabloid-reading tourist.

✍

(As when the eyes, after having been rubbed vigorously,
vine over with vessels. Or when an old photo half-
survives a flood. Or when, skimming through an old journal,
hasty entry, I read the word *memory* as *mommy.*)

✍

I was blown away. We long to be blown away, long
further and further back into the impossible
moment of our conception, our parents' spent bodies—

mine in a Washington D.C. cemetery (true)
scouring the ground for a contact my mother'd lost,
June, the cherry trees months past bloom, my father making
crayon rubbings of headstones, one in particular
that sounds like Donne ("Death, tho Thou art hungry, Thou shalt not
consume this man's memory") he kept and gave to me
along with his quirky ontological pensions,
good father leaning up from the ground, let's put him there,
on his back, with her on top, a few weathered petals
pasted to his skin, her knees, and bless their reverie—

without which we would not exist, the angel of life
making its entrance only when we're entranced, only
when our minds are so emptied, so dizzied free of will.

᠅

Isn't this how an image enters our minds, bucking
its way in, consciousness's clothing strewn about, tossed
into flowering rhododendrons, the ridiculous
premise of union suddenly possible—and then
after the jags, the thick pulsing, the pulling apart,
we repair once again, better or worse, to ourselves.

᠅

To the impression of it, that which we can barely
muster but muster we do. Memory of memory,
in that ill-lit room I lay silent listening but
for what? My mother to walk up the stairs carrying

a pot of stove-warmed water, a few steaming washcloths
draped around the edge. I know a kindness when I see it.

✃

Even when I couldn't see it well. Like the sumacs
from a distance: the poisonous-when-boiled seedpods
hovering as if unheld by their branches, umber flames
burning faintly out in the hands of a pending saint.

✃

If one were charged with tending them. If the mind with its
numberless palms in supplication weren't part mendicant,
part porch-light, part jam-jar, part groaning tree frog encased.

✃

If we weren't our own saints kneeling without modicum
assistance beside the mind's long-digested meals—

✃

Sleet and the quicksilvered world: back lawn ice-enameled.

Drone of John R traffic blending with cicada haze.

Brief tattoos of dock planks pressed into my back, boathouse
light cutting the school of shiners that first girl, looking
past my virgin shoulders, must have seen, have taken in.

My son arriving (a short eternity ago)
at the breakfast table holding his drawing, a few
crude green marker-made shapes—'Member this, Grama?, he said,
pointing. It's the moon. I can't touch it.

## SUSTENANCE

I tracked it through the one mind of the woods.
Its hoofprints pressed in snow were smallish hearts.
Buck-fawn: he let me come so near, take aim.
Crouched against a fir, I was anything.
Bush, stump, doe in estrus he could rut.
Not his maimer, though, not his final thought.
He stared me down until I shot him: low.
Then the forest forgot he'd ever been.
Nascent, there were signs: bonechip, spoor, frail hair.
But no memory, wounded, wants to die.
He hid in the dark timber, twice crossed the creek.
Finally he lay heaving out last breaths.
Dusk-cast shadow, he died where he was made.
A bite of heart sustains but is not him.

A friend's early death had me thinking about death,
as did the plastic toy stegosaur I ran over with the mower
when the sputtering engine and day's umber finality
had me thinking along similar lines. This is the way it goes
with death, I heard me telling myself in a voice I have
developed over the years to cope with such situations
though I don't trust so much as resign to it. C was crushed
while skiing the backcountry when a mid-June avalanche
unseated the peak he'd stared at from his kitchen window
several hours prior while fixing a breakfast
of toast and venison as the room filled with dawn's
initial hue and the slight hiss of butter losing its shape
in the skillet. What one does so early in the day is one's own
business—I delivered newspapers as a boy and prefer
to let a decent hour arrive before waking. Today though
Molly startled me at 4:37 screaming I want you, Daddy,
and as I held her until the offending dream gave way
to some less threatening vision, the eclipsing moon
I declined to set an alarm for appeared between the curtains:
as much moon as I have in my thumbnail, silver handle
by which some god held a pail filled with water drawn from
the cosmos's deepest well. I stepped outside in time to see
the vast mouth swallow all but the last slice of pear. Blood
rush of the creek, the robins' somnolent calls a deafening
surround to these thoughts, which a sizeable portion

of me would have preferred to sleep through, all but
the top of my head, the urnful I will be, buried warmly
under the quilts. Momentarily the snowy peak on which he left
his body arrived in daylight. Or daylight arrived on the peak.
They met, made a horizon line, and said nothing
of how at dusk in June up there one might see
a nighthawk drop from an invisible precipice, the edges
of its wings audibly sawing the ozone, slitting a seam
in the void into which he slipped.

## WINDOWSILL

Buff-colored moth, tracings
of wingscales on pane, ledger
of its last minutes—difficult
to tell death throes from vent lint.

When the goose fell dead at the bus stop, it was not quite dead (the hunter having taken a high shot because the goose would not decoy, the spreading wad of bismuth pellets shattering only the left phalange, barely piercing the breast), so when a plucky girl broke semicircle of wavering boys, reached to hoist the bird in her arms, its black head shot out hissing, its good wing flailed Icarus-like (though the children knew nothing of him yet), fanning gutter trash until the chocolate Lab arrived (stretching with each purposed stride the neoprene camo vest, scrotum bouncing, toenails clicking ridiculously on the cul-de-sac sidewalk) to clamp his jaws—after a brief scurry, stutter-flight—around the pillowed shoulders of the goose that was still not quite dead. Shotgun shouldered (afraid so), the hunter soon appeared, a tad portly, knelt and pried bird from beast's mouth, stroked the tooth-torn plumage, scratched his *good boy* behind the ear. Then twisted the bird's esophagus shut, stepping back from the throes as the bus (yellow, lethargic as a swath of mill-tinged dawn) climbed, crested the hill, and coasted to a curbside stop: its driver surveying the scene (*Tarnation*), releasing the brakes, filling the poised air with a collective gasp.

## WEEKLY APOCALYPTIC OR POEM WRITTEN
## ON THE WALL IN AN ASCENDING SPACE CAPSULE

We had to stop what we were doing
to see what we had done. Thing was
we wouldn't. How devoted we were
to despising one another, to erecting
our own private islands made of water
bottles and various other plastic
disposables. "Will you forgive me?"
was a phrase stricken from our language—
theirs too, "they" ballooning to include
nearly everyone but that arcane term
"us." Upon discovering that gulls
feasting on our dead but unearthed bodies
died of our toxicity, we sobered up
but couldn't stand to look at ourselves
in what was left of the light. Despite
what so many movies had taught us, just
in time was a tick too late. There was
this bird we used to call a whippoorwill.

*Birds here should have names so hard to say you name them over.* Someone dead wrote that, but yesterday watching the struggling flycatcher—Hammond's, Dusky, Willow, I'm not sure—I thought it. Beak pierced by some errant angler's snagged Gray Wulff, the bird flailed circles around a branch, the monofilament line coiling tighter with each brief orbit.

All this while you were teaching. Snow—in the first week of May!—then sunshine, then midges, then mayflies, then stones: the bugs' wrinkled wings like sheets a body has risen from, late for whatever it had to do. Mary, the warblers, tree swallows, the phoebes, feasted on the numb bugs, dashing down on the river, veering, their bellies white shirts beneath unbuttoned coats. Then snow again and the birds buttoned up, raced for the branches: your students, faces flushed, lined up after recess. All except Shannon, last again, out there playing tetherball alone. *It's May, sweetie, it's time for class.*

This morning studying the field guide I can't tell a Yellow-bellied from a Least, a Pewee from an Olive-sided. *Pip-pip,* I say there, sings one of them. *Pil-pil,* sings another, *ho-say ma-re-ah.* The bird that sang like it had swallowed too much water hung in the man-made gallows, and with the bow rope I broke the branch, with forceps pried the steel from its beak. It lit in a dogwood, bent-necked. The watery sound of the nothing it sang, friable thing gone from my palm. *May:* how a student slurring her words might say your name.

## THAT BLUE

That blue, almost cerulean, alchemical light
made when the full May moon appears near its apex
after the sun's just set: In it,

on a batholith between snowfields and snowfed river,

a sedan parked near the modest cemetery, a man
in denim work shirt and jeans, cowboy hat
hitched under an elbow. Hands in his pockets.

The river, as they say, is running off. To where, with what? To the last place current would carry a body if a body lay itself beside slipping banks, knelt even, and asked to be moved. Not the placid tour you might envision: having never seen mill pulp seeping acridly from settling ponds, having never seen the soles of young lovers' shoes through a footbridge's fenced floor. Having no idea how long a cliff-borne hydraulic could hold you under. I counted once, singing "I'll Fly Away" three times before the brutish swirl spit back the huge cedar it had swallowed with such nonchalance. I thought back then I wanted water, the great beast, flowing over and around me, wanted to be eroded, spread in flood across the sedge-lit bottoms: a stillness, in other words, the living aren't allowed.

A man I'd watched, though, named Dick Curran would faithfully ford the cold flow that winter in jeans, pulling braces of whitefish from the hole. Knock each head with his knife-handle priest and leave them lying atop the stones I wanted to be, glistening in the sun's midday stare. I knew it like a liturgy: the hunched figure squinting at the union of line and water until light quivered and man and river were likewise joined, just elements, forces of nature. Then by its tail he'd grasp the fish, split its skull. A nod, a wave to me across the riffle. Tipped hat. At certain moments of high stillness, I expected him to walk onto and across the water, the fish shuddering, slipping back. Of course he'd simply sit there on his bucket beneath the thin, glaucoma sky while my toes grew so cold I thought to offer them for bait.

We are just bait, he said the evening I found him sprawled out on the icy two-track, his scattered catch staring blindly up at the wide arcs of crows.

*Help me right here before they freeze*—and so we slit the bellies of those fish open, ran the roe out with our fingers. Then rode in the truck's warm silence to his basement room full of tackle, fillet knives, blades on the counter beside his crude oil landscapes: *Something to do,* he said pointing to the paintings, *to mark the days.* In essence what Santa Lucia said when asked why she carried her pocked-out eyes in a dish. Something to do while dodging the pimps she refused to whore for, or strolling across the Swedish countryside, cradling that bowl like a luminaria. A living half-testament—depending, of course, on the myth—to the scripture she often canted: *If the eyes are sound, the whole body is filled with light.*

Songless, Curran carried maggots beneath his tongue to keep them from freezing and a white bucket filled sometimes with fish he boiled and served with salt and lemon butter to the folks at Friendship Manor Retirement Center, and once to a young man who believed they existed only on ornate canvases, in baroque tales. Never saw him again, but read he died late one August: the river, predictably, low enough to cross.

## THEY TIED THE MADMEN TO TREES BESIDE THE RIVER
## AND ALL THE SHRINKS WENT OUT OF BUSINESS

When one day word got around that a man
lashed to the mast of a moored cottonwood (his arms
were allowed to flail about in the manner of the half-crucified)
suddenly stopped frothing and opened
the worn doors of his eyes—
                              April, the pileated woodpecker's
maniacal laugh deluged by the newly returned meadowlarks'
articulate description of moving water, the cottonwoods
despite all, opening again, scenting the trusted air—
                                            and began to:
he wasn't quite sure what, but guessed the river
had entered his body (made fistulous in months of wind) and found
a route out through his eyes. And untied, he floated (though
it was a long way and nothing migratory about it) wordlessly
beneath the dervish sky.

## GHAZAL IN WHICH END WORD
## REPETITION IS IMPLIED

The phone call comes at midnight.
The man walks outside weeping.

Making tea the next morning he sees through puffed
eyelids his discordant amblings in the snow.

How elliptical they are! As if some drunk
made them, or a stumbling injured animal.

For a while—and perhaps this is what the elders meant
by grace—he can even imagine he was not their maker.

*Who puts on boots and shuffles through a dusting,*
*falls to the ground, flails his arms and legs?*

Does not each day grant such meager detachment?
As if angels grab us underarm and briefly lift.

Just before the tea cools to the precise temperature
of a tear, and the cup, warm, weighs heavy in the hand.

Should be writing this with moths' wings, with water
on a rain-spattered stone. But here I am, a body
failing to behave with the discretion the spirit
has spent long years teaching it: Your closed eyes
are ampersands, meaning they stand for something
else. Meaning you don't watch as I describe them
or, from memory, what's behind the lids: dual
creeks taking separate draws down the same
mountain, two passages, two ungovernable
frontiers. *From memory?* When we were lost,
forced to sleep in the forest, my forlorn uncle
plucked the grouse we'd shot and lined our caps
with plumage. Two cages the light pries open
now. Meaning those birds whose wings I broke
long years ago flush defiantly out at me again.

## SEPTEMBER MINIATURES
## WITH BLOOD AND MARS

Even day
breaks

      *᷒᷒*

In the white bowl the grouse's blood
dries pink then vanishes in the warm
suddenly pinkish rinsing water.

      *᷒᷒*

Spiders had been sleeping in the logs I split,
fell curled to the chopping block and tumbled
drowsily into the grooves the maul had made,
oblivious to mercy.

      *᷒᷒*

Through a hole in the leaf, aphid-chewed,
the size of a dilated pupil: Aggins Peak
to which the first dusting clung
waiting for its next incarnation.

      *᷒᷒*

A niece told me she could hear fire
"crinkling" under the earth. Who's to say?
Alone here I find myself listening,
whispering when I speak at all.

      *᷒᷒*

Having determined Pascal's solution to all

problems (sit an hour with one's thoughts) impossible
I napped soundly in the hammock—a man
is more than his mind, sang Blind Willie
as did Dock Ellis tossing a no-hitter in 1970 while on LSD.

≈

Where did the day go? Now and then against
the tin siding of this trailer parked among
thistles, a last grasshopper: kicks; kicks; kicks.

≈

The boy asked—When we die, do our days
start over—then drew seven separate pictures
of ants, each numbered. Your ant companions.
Come home soon. Scooby Doo Band-Aid
stuck to the last page.

≈

After the storm
the firmament bled
and the blood
was light

≈

What ferryman brought us here across this black
nameless flow? Same one waits to float us
back across, his cigarette tip winking in the dark.

Just about anything'll whiten up. Cleaned a buck last week some guy's uncle
shot in 1952. Skinned the head, removed the tongue, detached the jaw to save
my beetles some work—three days it was white-white, beetle-bleached. Stink
a bit? The neighbors petitioned the health department twice, but I've lost my
sense of smell. When it's real bad my right eye waters. The wife asks do I want
chili or soup, but I can't taste the difference. Don't tell her. Just say chili one day,
soup the next. Brain's the first thing to decompose, but the beetles won't touch
it, so I use this gas-powered hose called the brain-blaster. And bone saws, duct
tape, plastic wrap, couple chemicals like magnesium carbonate. That's it. Plus
six million carrion bugs. They'll smell a carcass twenty miles away—the dead
get famous quick. Eat skin, fur, whatever you feed 'em. Feathers, hair, whiskers,
eyeballs, beards, tissue. Done some forensic work. Human hip bones, human
skulls. Had to go off the radar there. Under the table, you know? No favorites. If
forced to say? I guess that lynx skeleton chasing the skeleton of a snowshoe hare,
or that covey of Hungarian partridge hunched there, ready to flush. You know
the ground's made of bones, right, you're walking on bones. No more than
the next guy, I don't think. That rot there is the stench of life. As long as those
beetles don't peel off the carcasses and come crawling for me, I know my blood's
not cold. Hold your hands out. Both of them. Go on, reach toward it. Feel how
warm it is?

HAMMOCK POEM

What is the brain that it needs this occasional
cleansing, the gray nodes and branches imagined
as the pear tree's blossoming branches shifted by breezes
eons in the making.
                          Preempted by three bitter decades,
my troglodytic lament concluded an hour ago when god
promised to grant a wish I'd made at age eight
on a Thanksgiving wishbone—numb glee until I realized
that the actual request had slipped my mind and my anger
redoubled.
              What is scarier than the self?
                                          Home
is knowing where the spoons are and I couldn't find
a whisk, even feared the fork's shadow, which flushed me
from dinner to this rocking net, my mental intestines
having dined for too long on spoiled goods.


                                    Dear birds
of the tangled ceiling above, bestow upon me a droppingless
departure, clear the crooks and holds that this tree
might be a tree, aglow with the old prescription:
moon, pear blossoms.
                          This, that, and the day goes,
Issa would have said.
                          And did, regarding plums.

STUBBORN POEM

I wanted to write something as stubborn as the leaves
that refused to fall when October snapped so cold
but hung on like dour parchment all crumpled
through winter until February's first chinook

cast them off, one among the countless landing
on the creek's dense ice shelf on which I walked
one warm afternoon with Molly who pointed a small
finger at the loner that—darkening as it sponged up

the melt and warming as it soaked up the sun—had begun
to sink into the crust. Slowly, though. Like an anvil
falling through a fathom of unbearably blue sea. Sand
flaring in silence as the iron strikes sea floor. The leaf

looked a little like the black muscle as unmentionable in poetry
as poetry itself and while I pondered whether my own,
lifted and laid clear, would melt as deeply into the frozen
strata, Molly peeled it, the leaf, from the slush and held it

briefly against her cheek before folding it in two. She
dropped it into the hurtling riffle. How rare to touch
a child's reddening fingers and know the leaf
has let go its branch, that it is falling through the body

at its vague pace toward booted feet. It will sound,
settling, like a leaf lighting on water, or like the land
gasping as it does each late winter evening when
the sky at tree line, nearly sapphiric, goes black.

## NOSTRUMS (BILL MONROE)

*When a feller can play a banjo so well like that that it begins to make the cold chills run over you he can be doing you some good there I'm telling you* and the gentleman to my left here can strum a November midnight with the lodestar lone as a thumbprint on a frosty windowpane and make a G-chord yelp like a yard dog porcupine-quilled and left out to learn in deep snow, he might hold one note still as a bluebottle fly on a December sill then tick his way through a scale like a right fevered man, or sound a bass chord hollow as a dilapidated cabin procured by the wind as its instrument then fill you up with the next note warm as whiskey chased down with cold water straight from the spigot.

a distant city
barraged by twin-engine bombers, skyscraper flames
incarnadine half-masking a flock of white swans above
two glowering alligators (one soldier points his rifle
at the beasts while a second stands between them
frowning) harried by a single ill-defined flying object
which could be helicopter or archangel.

Although the irony is palpable, the irony is not the story.

I taught
the second graders knots two days before I found him, my only
son, hanging from his ceiling fan.

Some sound knocked me awake,
then the phone rang, his girlfriend sobbing (they'd been in a fight),
and I rose from the couch, my nursing textbook thumping on the
floor, to take him the portable.

I instruct CPR on weekends to
would-be lifeguards but couldn't pull him down, his sinews, once
taut from snowboarding, gone slack.

Who knows how the neighbor
heard my screams but he did and arrived to find me balancing on
the chair, taking some strain off the noose.

✍

Say you are sixteen and your father has another family, two sons
he doesn't call his sons but treats as such, and you live with your
mother who swallows your disdain like so many antidepressants
ignored in green bottles in your book bag.

But look at me now, lying on my
back, her lips latched to mine.

She's feeding me again, this time
with oxygen.

When I was in her body, when she prayed twice
daily to Saint Anne because she'd lost three already, she fed me

with fluids, her body tending the wavering flame of my heartbeat
that is passing now into the great vacancy and which she must
again retrieve from nothingness.

I wanted this quiet but not forever,
all the gatekeepers here, reverent to the silence.

I never imagined
lantern light so blue against running water.

Already, we're crossing,
the leeches and caddis huts loosed by our boots, the slow water
shallower than expected.

&

Comes to worse.

When I was a boy I feared most the bars on the
basement windows, the sound of the nighthawks' wings sawing
through the dusk, the placenta from sister's birth that my mother
buried in the garden, though now I'm sure that these readied me to
stare this moment in the eyes.

If and when a son is born, you can
cry, can weep openly when he dies, but when he is somewhere
vaguely in between, you had better fasten yourself to a sturdy
trunk, throw a loop around his legs, and bore your heels into the
earth.

I saw a girl walking to school today in her pink jacket
past the school playground where the wind was moving ever
so slightly the empty swings beneath a pine whose needles numbered
our myriad notions of God.

If you look up from an Internet article on comas from which you had learned that the largely inert head of a comet is also called a coma, you might just see such a thing.

⁂

As a girl I would become quite despondent when the liturgy closed with a hymn I didn't like because I knew the song would linger in my head throughout the day, eddying—yesterday I saw while driving to the hospital a wet barn in dusk, and cannot close my eyes today without its afterimage singeing the backs of my eye lids.

Yes, it was red; it had rained for the briefest of moments.

⁂

I'm fingering the tatters of a dream-scarf that unraveled just as I took hold of it: Coming home through the backyard in the 3 a.m. rain toward the single lit window peppered with a million spent moths, I stumble on my old dog Valley who straightens her front legs, a hint she might rise up to greet me, then falters with dramatic sigh, a long exhalation that threatens to be her last: *No you don't*, I tell her, *no you don't*.

⁂

Coffee, green tea, some carb-free ginseng smoothie: each morning you pour it, you drink from your cup of blame, and it's good because at least then you can stop thinking, stop talking causalities around it.

When he was three and his mom and I were still together we visited her relatives back east and driving home late one night stopped to see Niagara Falls.

You forget that it's a river, I mean
before it takes that sheer drop, it's just a river meandering between
its banks.

       Cold or afraid, he climbed up onto my chest and I zipped
him inside of my coat—my major foray into this welter of self-pity
is not that it's all gone but that it's all left.

๛

I could blame the bookshelf with its Camus and Berryman but each
one of us except the most calloused or the most genetically attuned
has dreamt of a riverbank cut deep enough to bury us, an impact
with enough dominion to annihilate that madness.

                               Forever,
whatever forever means.

                I would have envisioned blaming myself
a little more—if only I'd packed him a slice of carrot cake, if only
the concert, if only the—but the conditional tense is not conducive
to survival, which tells me he's still with us.

                         I can only wish him
more earth, in the bluntest of terms: another stolen swig of whiskey
brief as a July snow, another hard tumble on his board, another
fuck, another hummingbird.

๛

I can't see them, but I know their voices, the sweet slightly fecal
scent of dying lilacs, the sound of coins sliding back in the pocket
of my father sitting down in a chair, birdsong they haven't opened
the window to yet: omens all.

I am alive to think but barely mutter
that the river of myth was as wet as any other, bride of fire: cold,
then very cold, until it turns hot.

They can keep your light on but
they haven't figured out that you can hear the television tuned to a
documentary on wolverines, a trapped animal bashing itself against
the live-trap's lid weighed down by two hundred-pound sandbags,
and the intern's story one night about a stillborn the doctor
delivered feet first, head they delivered the woman of.

Thus I am
wombed away again, sleeping this not-sleep, wondering if I'll
arrive again in the wakefulness that seemed so often like a dream.

∽

In the beginning there was a boy sleeping in his bed and in the end
there'll be a boy sleeping in his bed, and here in this between there
is a boy—when I call him mine I weep—sleeping in his bed.

∽

A few stray notes get left out of the fugue but of course I can't
remember what they were: did I say the mark the noose left
covered up the hickey I had chastised him about, that the noose
itself was his beloved yellow belaying rope?

My favorite poet
wrote *the scent of dying lilacs reminds the soul that it exists* so
yesterday I cut a hundred boughs from the bushes (this tells me it's
almost May) and placed them in jars around his room, the blooms
the color of his face when I found him.

In the warrens of grief, no way appears that does not hint at why you entered.

～

I came to wailing last night and now am certain that what I thought was shallow water rushing over stones, the current embracing my tightening form, was really mother-hush, her small arms holding me a little longer here.

Mother, you are a brief spring snow and the ash's berry clusters not quite blushing.

～

Late last August a torrid thunderstorm caught us just upstream from Triple Bridges and I remember thinking, as the boat slipped beneath each bridge between the thin sheets of water pouring from each high edge: mercy might be brief but it is mercy.

I didn't say amen: I would compose my prayers—take him from this world, no, leave him here—but like an email deemed too personal, refused to hit the send button.

I recalled a bedtime story in which the boy who was to become the father of the boy to whom the story was being told by the narrator a cat, dupes an attacking rhino by giving it a toothbrush.

Why a toothbrush I haven't the frailest idea, but I understood just now, while the eyelids of the boy to whom I once read this story fluttered, that the fictional boy's only failing would have been to deem insufficient what he carried.

I see the edge of his
eyeball, squid-white, and don't know to whom these words go out
but whisper: That was kind of you.

The wind buffeting my eardrum.

There's a feeling I'd forgotten.

## FEBRUARY SIDEREAL
## WITH BACKYARD DOE

Sunday afternoon starlight
through the just-eaten apple's
core resting on the loveseat's
arm near mine. Same plenary
beam mints Ed's yellow siding
the color of cleaved lodgepole
and teases out each ridgeline
pine with the sharp teeth of its
billion-mile-long pocket comb.
But don't tell my thatch of dark
hair, grand narcissist gulping
this warmth as grass does the melt,
all the countless backyard stems
opening their mouths to meet
water's soft lips, to be met
some day soon by the young doe's
stern molars. Watching her work
old browse I note precisely—
wishing I could stop myself
from knowing that freedom
is nothing but the distance
between hunter and hunted—
where a hurtling piece of lead
would need to meet the subtle

crease behind her front shoulder
to kill her where, luminous,
she stands, and, standing with this
massive irony, feel light
strike the bones caging off my
own vitals. In the book of
illuminations, a page
falls upon a page, its edge
thin as the lustrous strand
binding us here, each to each,
keen as the dispatching blade.

## STILL LIFE WITH STARLIGHT

Nightborne, easterly, cumulus
catacomb the dawn—is he in

or out? If he had his druthers?
Down here no wind (or is the wind

still?)—down here in this lack of wind
the sure fork of aspen branches

like a divining rod with no quiver
above his head. No tilt. Stars

draining in their sockets, faint
maw-speech of geese falling

quiet as stardust, as the mountains
he's made of, to his ears. Eider

or weather-breath, what brushes
his bare neck, he wonders who

it thinks it is, touching him like that?

## STUDY FOR ACRYLIC OF SLEEMAN PEAK DUSK
## WITH WILDFLOWERS

Slightest wind in the pine's apexes: the lodgepoles
look to feel it more than do the firs but from inside
who can say for sure? Slope-clinging prairie smoke in tight purple
polyps, a few modestly bloomed *Castilleja*—

Latin for Indian Paintbrush
which struck me too ironic since I'm imagining a painting but
lacking the improvisational flourish of my son, three, who asks
for another canvas, butcher paper, really, before his last,
Landscape with Bush, Badger, and Fence Line, is even dry—

inlaid
with several parchment-dry irises folding pulselessly
into themselves, all amidst a wave of balsamroot climbing
horizon-ward like meerschaum retreating (who doesn't tire
of grandness? Gilbert: *I don't believe in modesty in the arts*)
with all the shoreline's light.

Some of the boy's sweet arrogance
here, please, his shrug at an uncle's compliment: *Oh that, that's
an airplane but I don't like it so much:* the old botanist's
indifference that the bloom was named for him: *I'm dying
in Spain and they dishonor a wildflower with my name!*

Their desire:
a vanishing point into which most properly the painter
disappears, impalpably as the elucidating if not incriminating dusk.

POEM WITH SEVERAL KEATSIAN REFERENCES,
POEM BURNING UP IN THE FIRE I LIT TO
WARM MY SON, OR DO AS I SAY NOT AS I DO

Given the circumstances, who wouldn't
talk to the birds—they can fly, we can't.
I fancy starting out flirtatiously as with
this predawn phoebe: "Hello, darkling,
where've you been all my life?" Sure,
when we say *the world* we're merely hedging
guesses but I'll take a stab this morning,
I'll buzz in: I recall one glorious fall hunt
when I stumbled for the scantest of moments
into a response to Blind Willie Johnson's
earnest query "What is the soul of a man?"
before the pheasant of an answer flushed
properly into a windy horizon. When young
I drew a picture of an orange and purple
monster which my mother captioned with
what must have been my words—"This is
Chee-Chee, he's a spider ranger, he steals
souls"—long before I was told they didn't
exist (monsters, souls). But I've witnessed
the monster I can be drawn by my own
young son, cobalt blue with yellow eyes
labeled by his preschool teacher "a scary
person who isn't really a person," so I think

I'll keep my soul this morning, a consolation
prize, fledgling my mother once nourished
with a pot of stove-warmed water carried
to a tepid bath, hence my first thought
while looking out the predawn window:
*the moon as a pot of stove-warmed water*
*your mother carried to your tepid bath*, hence
my conclusion that perhaps good John Keats
was wrong, that the world isn't the vale
of soul-making so much as it is the river
running through the vale in which souls
can drown. I knew I was flailing when
yesterday a sparrow landed next to me
in the grocery store parking lot and I
had nothing to say to it, whereas when
my young son ate boot-slush off the doormat
I yelled, sent him without a bath to bed
though he shook from the gouts of ice
that slid melting down his gullet. Since when
had I become a wiggler unworthy of a bait-hook
squirming on the shanty floor, I wondered, my negative
capability increasing through the night until the boy
woke crying, the woodstove fire dead.

　　　　　　　　—some frigid mornings the snow
fell sideways instead of down, striking your cheek
with countless pinpricks, as if the world wanted
inside of you. If wind blew off the lake, white clumps
formed in the crooks of branches, eggless nests,
birdless too, small brains the gusts dismantled: thought
extinguished, falling and aglimmer. Evenings we skied
across the lake towing the boy behind us in the sled,
poorer than we'd ever been, the lake beneath the ice
a deep shadow of the ice—tell me that line again, she'd ask
—*bluish, associating with their shadows*—
and happier too. At dusk a single shanty lantern,
faintly, first; at dawn the same disappearing into day,
light on light. Often from a stone building's open
windows students rehearsed solos, and oboe notes
floated toward us as if on parasols, and once the young
cellist from Japan, who looked always like she'd been
crying, met us on the path and bent to place her earphones
in the boy's ears: *Puccini,* she said, flakes collecting,
melting in his lashes. Wraiths of snow, brittle leaves
sketching their way to rest; more weeks of wet wool,
flannel, snowsuits steaming up the window whose frame
bled groggy ladybugs, droplets from unseen veins. Then,
without harbinger, a dawn with the scent of the Gulf in it,
rumors of warmth urging schools of mint fish into shallows

to wait for rain at the creek's threshold. The thaw begun:
brusque aubade, no kiss for the snow from the roof, just
a gentle shrug and the gutters spilling over. Three straight
days. The eaves thrumming until the sun appeared
like a ghost whose presence no one questioned. Walked
down to the morphing shoreline to bathe in this warmth
with the nymphs wriggling through slush and an ice fisherman
jigging, on the punk ice, from his bucket, for smelt, his bait
twisting in the liquid dark beneath him like a seed.

# FLUVIAL

Comes cauldroning up the canyon
masking the trestles and docked railcars,
unlit offices and quiet exits
of custodians, just-wakened dogs steaming piss
into the frost-lacquered grass: Riverfog,
the valley brimming over. This daily miracle
must be breathed—so cold even the rash crows
bark reverently—to be believed. Afternoons
the hood lifts a little and great cumulus come steepling eastward,
cutting through fog and country: the mountains again,
seen as through old glass, ridgeline ponderosas wind-pardoned,
surviving worshipers of the sky. Without which we—
the woman (for instance) the man opens his door to,
her white shirt-collar wet, short hair
still dripping: she'd just wrung it out, droplets
like mercury down her soft forearm—would have nothing
so sufficiently void of us, from which our mark's been so erased:
beyond the clouds—mute isolations, always our innerworkings—
and beyond that beyond. High geese
like a long muted chain of twisting keys
fly into it, the easy locks turning but the blue
restitute: unturnable page the nearsighted below
can't make out. Though water—even puddles, little avatars—brings it
near. And just as hard to grasp,
small epiphanies falling through the fingers: of a girl

bent above the clogged sewer grate, pocking

her cirrus-couched portrait, staring until the face is restored,

until the school bus whines to a stop . . . and later the pool

fills with the strange rain of stars. . . . And even later,

because I am—because the water in me is urged

by prostrate hills, summoned, I go to you

who I have called, from the willow-stitched islands and suicide bridges

without a trace of threnody, scores

of insufficient names: earth's eye, marrow of the valley,

handleless blade, huskless body, moon's

ossuary, gouge, Our Father of Eternal Current, Holy

Mother of Arsenic and Lead, pallbearer of shopping carts and condoms,

hobos' lullaby, lamp of the body of the beloved,

River of Nothing, O Inextinguishable—

blue flame beside which I am irreparably knelt.

THE ROOFERS LISTEN TO HEART'S
"CRAZY ON YOU" AS THEY WORK

compression-stapling gravel shingles to angled beams
to keep the coming rains out (*Thanks, I rather liked the
syllable-at-a-time conversation the leak was
having with the bucket*)—late November's agate-light

crazing on the worn steel of belt-hooked hammers, honed points
of teeth-held nails. One face hums falsetto through asbestos grit,
"Wild man's world is cryin' in pain, what you gonna do
when everybody's insane," and free hands air-pick synthesized guitar,

notes vaulting over the peak onto the coveralled men
like warm wind. Like the last of it. Is this not the work
of the one who sent us? My work is wonder, which has for too long
seemed a distant season. But it's winter now: Is this hymn—

"So afraid of one who's so afraid of you / What else
you gonna do / Let me go crazy on you"—not in Thy book?
I would never have looked for it there, assuming what moved me
moved you, knowing little of cathedrals before today.

## VESPERS BEGINNING AS SHEEP TALLOW
## IN THE HANDS OF A PRIEST

*St. Ignatius, Montana, 1856*

No less important than the light
is what it falls on: penitent coil of wick
rising from clay floor to scraps of tallow

shaped into the candle hung (bare wall,
three nails, the casual horror of the iron)
beside a window open this spare March evening

to homeward geese, their mist-parting calls, a rainfrock
above mountains we named Mission
for the building we built beneath them.

By now it's another life's list: a pasture
veiled in frost where a frost-colored mare
lowers her head to graze; a kite without a wind

to fill it; the quilt laid across my mother (its blue
of washed and sunbaked stones) whose wheezing
kept time with the rocking chair the plump

monsignor always chose, his Saint Louis habit
of talking at great lengths about books he'd never
read; her dress hanging still wet on the line, mothlit

as I prayed her passage was; brotherless,
keeperless, a blackbird flying so quickly west
the coming, evening sky fails to darken.

I live beneath these mountains, as if
beneath the stoppage of time: snow-blanketed
distance, the clouds' one encumbrance.

As if beneath the last statues worthy
of adoration, the remaining uncorrupted,
snow gathered atop them as on

the shoulders of the dead. And these tribes,
the dying dead-to-be: I pray they seal up those things
uttered by the seven tongues and write them not,

for we novitiate have failed to learn,
even with the fat of the Lamb on our hands,
any of their rectitude. Even with the valley's light

lapidary in the canyon creases, the two rivers
joining limpidly.—*If God is for us,*
*who can be against us?* Besides God?

Blackberries straight from the unsprayed vines.
And far below beneath the sheer dune's scarp
the huge swaying horizontal swath of ocean
tilting at some uncharted point to adjoin
a vertical wall of cumulus—this could be
Dover, some dolorous place to which the woebegone
journeys and offers himself up to the palatable
salt and brome. But the small family has the red
overlooking cottage (black shutters) on loan
and has spent the fogged-in morning picking
the alternately tart and ripe-sweet fruits: the boy,
just three, plopping one after another in his
yellow plastic wagon while the woman and man
fill emptied coffee cups. Faint sexual suggestion
of the berries' texture on the tongue. Gull cries
cast into and slicing gull-like through wind, sudden
white eruptions below (whale-spouts!) inaudible
but the crashing-back nonetheless imaginable
as the mammal's barnacled flukes. Shivering,
but not from cold, the boy asks for a second
breakfast, and inside she pours him cornflakes topped
with berries onto which the man heaps a scoop
of ice cream: a radiant look of surprise, milk
beswirled with wines and purples. Small, sparing bites
from a single cold-lipped spoon. The kitchen slants,

she notes, to the north, down the hill, up the coast.
Backing away, he crops a far-off haystack butte
from the window, frames just their faces, and water,
the great revisionist. Last loud scoops from a titled
bowl, and soon the boy is napping with a baffling
alacrity. How long had it been since he'd fallen
asleep with the weight of his son on his chest?
He eases open, pulls closed the door, touches
her shoulder: there's a quiet bed upstairs, he's
tested it; she closes her slim but lauded novel,
grins. Straits-light on the sheets—she's barely
pregnant: straits-light on her barely swelling belly
unseen by the unseen child. Their love is a boy
eating berries and ice cream for lunch. Afterward,
her flanks falsely bruised from where his stained fingertips
had touched her, they awake to rain, plaits of shade
moving on them long after they've stopped to wonder
when these arrived, not joy, but the more
forbidden and fleeting: happiness, and straight
as a ladder leaned precariously against a shake-
shingled roof, the dense rainbow slanting up from sea.

However arrogant I had to be
to say something like, It's what a poem is, I was,
while you honed a beech branch end
and with it clinically stabbed four hot dogs asking
did I remember the ketchup.
You didn't trust me? No—certainly not enough
to let me cook the franks, wrapped now
in the bluish flames, skins splitting open, charring—
for fear I might turn the meal,
you said, taking the first, juice-spitting bite, into
a metaphor, and you were hungry.

## NAÏVE MELODY

Some photos I cannot hold without kissing—
this one spilled from the pages of a book
like an aster whose petals, drying there,
infused the words they were pressed between
with a white so vivid the novel's droll
protagonist walked out of his dark midday bar
blinking at a lavish alpine meadow though
it had been December in Flint. A freckle
like a photo is a text the light's helped write
which explains why my friend told the kind
physician that he'd sooner lick the scalpel than
let her scrape six melanomas from his facial
canyons—forty-odd years ago sunlight
prisming on the Adriatic planted those crass
moles in place, and I can still feel it, he said,
bronzing my cheeks. He knew death was
a wind searching the back of his hand, veins
branching like his childhood sycamore leafed out
in liver spots, the trunk, its scaly bark, too steep
for memory to climb. But he stared at it anyway
and was somewhere other than that antiseptic
room. Just as I holding this glossy conjury
am no longer in the chair where dawn found me
tending my grief in the softening dark. I'm lying
in June grass looking up at her, she's two—

when I go to where he was in those late days
bring me flowers to kiss, hands to press
between pages, bring—Molly laughing, laughing,
Molly with the sun in her mouth.

GROVE

Labyrinthine,
      lanky-stemmed,
            dew-magnified;
sermonless,
      naked, aphid chewed,
            whiskered;
debtless,
      solipsistic, stained
         with sparrow droppings;
wind-ruddering, spared
      from squirrels' nests, diseased,
         quixotic;
turned away from rain, squatters,
      hangers-on about to be
         unhinged:
            prodigal the leaves
the earth accepts.

High mid-September summer afternoon:

                              Blessed art thou

among fruit flies, amber one, orbiting an incision in the ripe pear's skin
put there by our daughter's two bottom teeth.

                                    Whetted

the blade that shaves granular layer away,
slices a sliver of frost, wafer of sweet milk,

                              and blessed

the water falling from the tap, brief silver creek
coursing down forged slope,

                       ditto the white towel, belt-hung,

run tautly down the edge.

                     ❧

*Thud-ud:* in the thatchy
backyard grass: a fallen fruit, the old tree
burdened with herself.

                    *Thud:* another

the deer will chew in moonlight, their rough
tongues elastic, slathered in the juices,
their molars crushing meat and stem,

                            and moonlight.

*Thud-ud:* one more,

               as the black muscle hangs between its beats.

                     ❧

The high mid-September summer afternoon?
My spell to make it stay began: Earwig
staring up from sink-drain precipice with pinchers flared,
clasp me to this impossible hour
in which two yellowjackets have bored
so far into a fruit they rive the meat
from core;
           or cleave me from it like a boy's voice
sent-off from his body: my son's
coming on the cooling evening air,
                   a bird
among birds and calls of birds and quiet between bird calls—
mostly what I want is to keep
letting his words build their improbable nest
of sunlight inside the condemned warehouse
of my chest:
           *Is that what your eyes look like?* (My eyes welling.)
*I think they look like rivers.*
                 Write that down.
How does a boy muster a king's courage
amidst all this?
            All this what?
                 Not what the man
in the white suit said (*stay off the fertilizer*
*it's not poisonous but you shouldn't touch it*
*for six days*) but his schoolmate
pressing on the window screen

and falling three straight stories down and—

                                   *What means die?*

You know what it means, Love.

                           What kind of cowardice

answers that way a boy who, returning from the memorial, asked
*Is the moon following us? Is the moon*
*a shining thing?*

                Stay for sunrise.

                        What can't get said

gets wept.

                  ᕽ

In the house of an instant of seeing
I found upon the mantle: light
bled onto the valley floor, as if cloud,
rafter-hung, had been slit open,

                     or the ground

been gutted,

         and the gore of all those buried too soon
were seeping from the earth like so much strange moss
blooming from a desert's faux oasis
where literal bodies fertilize the chaff—

                             You've

hung a deer before. Everyone around here has
at least helped out:

              the eyes go blue and the tongue
slips from the jaw like a terrible pink jelly, the hide
peels effortlessly away leaving

its former bearer steaming, turning clockwise on its taut rope,
counterclockwise above its fate-turned-butcher
us—
      You were talking about the light?
                                  I am.
In the blood of which—of whom?—we are washed.

                    ☙

Nothing like seeing the dead boy's mother
to stifle the pre-game barbershop banter: Day
speechless, concussed.
                Tear-hoarder,
how high would you like your sideburns clipped
as she walks by the tinted window towing her
trailer of grief U-Haul couldn't quite provide insurance for,
                                        would you
wave, were your hands not folded under the silver apron
covered in shavings black and stiff as long-held childhood
silvers:
            Remember the pool-bound bugs, the bees'
honey-colored wings trapped and trapping prisms,
bark of a dog left outside all day, deep whunk
of Josh Levine diving in for quarters, someone's sister's
perked nipples unbearably close beneath a black sun-shellacked
suit—
            would you offer these, which her child will not know
in this life, like some strange bouquet for her table
full of bouquets, along with your fear-stained

self-pity—

*Would you like the sides*
*a little tighter?*

the scissor-filled old hands framing
your reflected head next to the reflected clock whose numbers:
Aren't backward?

*You've never seen*
*a barber's clock before?* he says. Spins you around to see
the referent, its numerals inverted, all too truer
representation of the hours' ruse.

～

They steam in the sere first frost, turds
like piles of lacquered raisins.

As opposed to?

To

summer's wonderfully forgivable boredom
and some vague pining for a female godhead,
the worms and millipedes watching the moon
about to sprout like a sudden hope
cajoled by the boy's present footwear:
oven mitts.

*The grass is fire*
*but I can't feel it.*

Wind tapers—up there
it moves great masses of moisture, down here
an eyelash—grief too?

I have heard some days she can't

open her pain-cottered mouth, a furnace
behind it leaking out the eyes.

                              Mother of god,
how did she hold in her arms the dead
fruit of her womb—and yours, of what did his lips taste,
plum-wine, that Sepphorian blood of yours?

                    ✑

In dark times I dream of women and they are you,
radiant as the countless flecks of gentian pollen
aloft in these unfinishable shafts of sun, a dominion
of dust.

            Of ash. Because doesn't it have to burn
before it can be restored?

                    The tree is aflame:
its fruit the color of its leaves the color of the light
they sift, nudged subtly by rusts, cinnabars
where the flame burns purest. Fallen swart November
leaves will make the ground above the roots seem
scorched:

            Shelve her eyes until then, in a box
lined with dark velvet, you who never thought
*One shouldn't have to do this* rather *There are many things
one shouldn't have to do,* sequester her ears
from this well-meant half-empathy, until the seeds
burst whitely in the earth. Seeds sewn on wind,
or in the droppings of a fawn.

A TOAST

Milkweed pod
gone to seed,
                                      pried
open, wind-
emptied:
                    two shallow
cups of shadow—

# NOTES

The title of this collection, "Earth Again," is taken from a section title in Czeslaw Milosz's "The Garden of Earthly Delights."

"Vespers Beginning as Sheep Tallow in the Hands of a Priest" borrows "the casual horror of the iron" from George Oppen.

"Comes to Worse" lifts "my major foray into this welter of self-pity" from Thomas McGuane. The bedtime story the father's voice refers to late in the poem is *My Father's Dragon* by Ruth Stiles Gannett.

"February Sidereal with Backyard Doe" reconstructs a phrase by Bei Dao.

"May": The opening sentence is from Richard Hugo.

"Wintering": The italicized phrase is from Elizabeth Bishop's "At the Fishhouses."

"Trimmings" borrows "the black muscle" from Denis Johnson and "the house of an instant of seeing" from Czeslaw Milosz.

*※*

"Tablet" is for Jeffrey Foucault.

"Brief Dream of Bronwyn Rae" is for John Roberts.

"They Tied the Madmen to Trees beside the River and All the Shrinks Went Out of Business" is for Christopher Howell.

"Partial Eclipse / N 46.677 W 114.244" is for Laurie Ashley and dedicated to the memory of Chris Spurgeon.

"Study for Acrylic of Sleeman Peak Dusk with Wildflowers" is for Phil and Julie Gardner.

ACKNOWLEDGMENTS

Many thanks to the editors of the following publications in which some of these poems previously appeared:

*Beloit Poetry Journal*: "Tablet," "A Toast"
*Carolina Quarterly*: "Small Fire in Snow"
*Cab (Conversations Across Borders)*: "Partial Eclipse / N 46.677, W 114.244,"
    "February Sidereal with Backyard Doe"
*Dunes Review*: "Wintering"
*A Face to Meet the Faces: An Anthology of Contemporary Persona Poetry*:
    "Nostrums (Bill Monroe)"
*Greatcoat*: "Fluvial"
*Grove Review:* "In the Weeks Before You Were Born, Driving through the
    Mission Valley, He Watches Her Begin a List for Labor"
*Guernica*: "Poem with Several Keatsian References, Poem Burning Up in the Fire
    I Lit to Warm My Son, or Do as I Say Not as I Do"
*Gulf Coast*: "Comes to Worse"
*Interlochen Review:* "May"
*Michigan Quarterly Review*: "Naive Melody"
*Neo*: "Blown Snow," "They Tied the Madmen to Trees beside the River and All
    the Shrinks Went Out of Business," "Vows"
*New Orleans Review*: "Vespers Beginning as Sheep Tallow in the Hands of a
    Priest," "Tarnation"
*Poetry*: "Sustenance"
*Orion*: "Possible Psalm"
*Seneca Review*: "I Canonize Dick Curran"

*Strange Machine*: "Inscription"

*The Sun:* "Weekly Apocalyptic or Poem Written on the Wall in an Ascending
　　Space Capsule"

Some of these poems also appeared in a limited edition chapbook, *September
Miniatures with Blood and Mars*, published by Checker Press. My gratitude to
Mason Miller for his artistry in this endeavor.

Deep thanks to:

Joyce Bahle, John Bateman, Tanya Cohen, Todd Davis, Mike Delp, Bob DeMott,
Rich Dombrowski, Jack Driscoll, Peter Drake, David Duncan, Jeffrey Foucault,
Hannah Fries, Dan Gerber, Sarah Gridley, Jim Harrison, Matt Henderson,
Joanna Klink, Melissa Kwasny, Dan Lahren, Helen McLean, Molly McNulty,
Jefferson Miller, Anne-Marie Oomen, Mika Perrine, Al Pils, Jack Ridl, Meredith
Rutland, Rob Schlegel, Doug and Anne Stanton, Pearl Smith, Carly Squires,
Brent Taylor, and David Warnock.

Also: Steve and Kinza, Bob and Jo, Jason and Gita, Tim and Lindsay, Steve and
Sally, Phil and Julie, Eric and Liz, Elke and Paul, Nick and Robin, Josh and
Steph, Tobe, Al, John.

Immense gratitude to Annie Martin.

May.